JUN -- 2010

Planets

Lynn M. Stone

Rourke
Publishing LLC
Vero Beach, Florida 32964

www.rourkepublishing.com

PHOTO CREDITS: All images © NASA; except for pages 6, 7, 9, 11, 13, 15, 17, 19, 20: © GEORGE TOUBALIS; page 8: © Varina and Jay Patel

Editor: Meg Greve

Cover and Interior designed by: Tara Raymo

Library of Congress Cataloging-in-Publication Data

Stone, Lynn M.
  Planets / Lynn Stone.
      p. cm. -- (Skywatch)
Includes index.
ISBN 978-1-60472-295-6 (Hardcover)
ISBN 978-1-60472-956-6 (Softcover)
1. Planets--Juvenile literature. I. Title.
QB602.S77 2009
523.4--dc22
                                        2008024850

Rourke Publishing
Printed in the United States of America, North Mankato, Minnesota
111309
111309LP-A

TABLE OF CONTENTS

Planets 4

Inner Planets .6

Outer Planets 12

Dwarf Planets 20

Glossary 23

Index 24

Planets

Mercury Venus Earth Mars Jupiter

Ceres

A planet is a massive body that travels in an **orbit**, or path, around a star. The planets in our **solar system** orbit the Sun, which is the nearest star.

Saturn

Uranus

Neptune

Pluto

Eris

Planetary Fact Box ★

- Number of planets: 8
- Number of dwarf planets: 3
- Other orbiting objects: moons, asteroids, meteoroids, and comets

A planet must also have a powerful gravity, or pulling force. The planets in our solar system are either **terrestrial** or **gas**.

5

INNER PLANETS

The four inner planets are: Mercury, Venus, Earth, and Mars.

Mercury

Mercury, the smallest planet, is closest to the Sun.

Planetary Fact Box

- Placement from the Sun: first
- Distance from the Sun: 36 million miles (58 million kilometers)
- Surface: terrestrial
- Number of moons: none
- Planetary year: 88 Earth days

Venus

Venus is nearly the same size as the Earth. Seen from Earth, Venus is the brightest object in the sky other than the Sun and Moon.

- Placement from the Sun: second
- Distance from the Sun:
  67.2 million miles
  (108.2 million kilometers)
- Surface: terrestrial
- Number of moons: none
- Planetary year: 225 Earth days

The Earth is the largest of the four inner planets. It is the only planet in the solar system known to support life.

Planetary Fact Box

- Placement from the Sun: third
- Distance from the Sun: 93 million miles (149.6 million kilometers)
- Surface: terrestrial
- Number of moons: one
- Planetary year: 365 Earth days

Mars is also known as the Red Planet because its soil contains **iron**. Scientists have searched without success for life on Mars using spaceships and land rovers.

OUTER PLANETS

The outer planets include Jupiter, Saturn, Uranus, and Neptune.

Jupiter

Jupiter's red spot is wider than three Earths.

Jupiter is the largest planet in the solar system. A great red spot on its surface is really a giant storm.

Planetary Fact Box ★

- Placement from the Sun: fifth
- Distance from the Sun:
  483.6 million miles
  (778.3 million kilometers)
- Surface: gas
- Number of moons: 63 (known)
- Planetary year: about 12
  Earth years

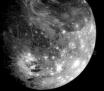

Saturn

Saturn is the farthest planet we can see without a telescope.

Saturn, the second largest planet, is famous for its **planetary rings**.

- Placement from the Sun: sixth
- Distance from the Sun:
  886.7 million miles
  (1,427 million kilometers)
- Surface: gas
- Number of moons: 56 (known)
- Planetary year: about 29
  Earth years

Uranus

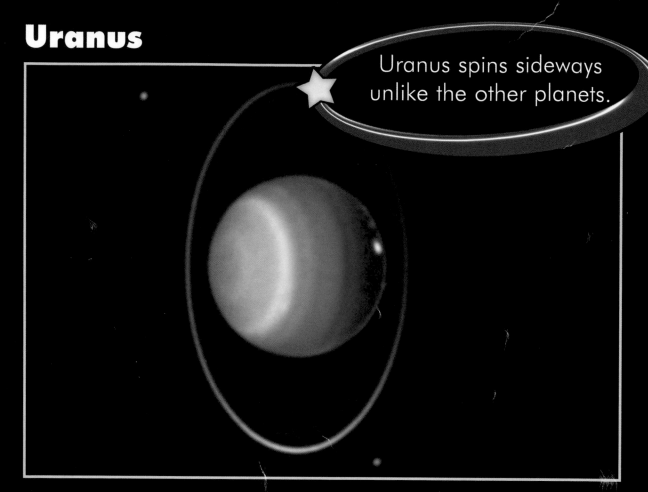

Uranus spins sideways unlike the other planets.

Freezing cold Uranus is the third largest planet. Methane gas gives Uranus its blue-green color.

Planetary Fact Box

- Placement from the Sun: seventh
- Distance from the Sun:
  1,784 million miles
  (2,871 million kilometers)
- Surface: gas
- Number of moons: 27 (known)
- Planetary year: 84 Earth years

Neptune

The great dark spot is a storm which resembles Jupiter's great red spot.

Neptune is the smallest of the outer planets and the farthest planet from the Sun.

- Placement from the Sun: eighth
- Distance from the Sun:
  2,794 million miles
  (4,497 million kilometers)
- Surface: gas
- Number of moons: 13 (known)
- Planetary year: 165 Earth years

DWARF PLANETS

Pluto, Ceres, and Eris are dwarf planets.
All three are smaller than the other planets.

Ceres

Eris

Pluto

What is the Difference?

	Planet	Dwarf Planet
Orbits the Sun	⭐	⭐
Strong gravity gives it a ball shape	⭐	⭐
Clears objects out of its orbit	⭐	

Scientists have discovered more than a hundred planets outside of our solar system. In the future, we might even be able to visit one!

GLOSSARY

gas (GASS): matter such as air that is not a liquid or a solid

iron (EYE-urn): a metal that turns red when it rusts

orbit (OR-bit): a circular path followed by one object in space as it travels around another object in space

planetary rings (PLAN-eh-taree RINGS): bands of dust and other matter that orbit the outermost major planets: Jupiter, Saturn, Uranus, and Neptune

solar system (SOH-lur SISS-tuhm): the Sun and those objects in space bound to it by gravity

terrestrial (tuh-RESS-tree-uhl): refers to the ground, or to that which is hard and solid

23

InDEX

gravity   5

iron   10

life   8, 10

methane   16

orbit   4, 21

planetary rings   14

water   8

FURTHER READING

Clifford, Tim. *Space*. Rourke, 2008.

Kerrod, Robin. *Jupiter*. Lerner, 2003.

Kerrord, Robin. *Uranus, Neptune, and Pluto*. Lerner, 2003.

WEBSITES TO VISIT

http://www.frontiernet.net~kidpower/astronomy.html

http://solarsystem.nasa.gov/kids/index.cfm

http://www.esaKIDSen/Planetsandmoons.html

ABOUT THE AUTHOR

Lynn M. Stone is a widely-published wildlife and domestic animal photographer and the author of more than 500 children's books. His book *Box Turtles* was chosen as an Outstanding Science Trade Book and Selectors' Choice for 2008 by the Science Committee of the National Science Teachers' Association and the Children's Book Council.

24